A WHEEL WITHIN A WHEEL

Frances E Willard

A WHEEL WITHIN A WHEEL

HOW I LEARNED TO
RIDE THE BICYCLE

WITH SOME REFLECTIONS BY THE WAY

BY

FRANCES E. WILLARD

Illustrated

APPLEWOOD BOOKS
BEDFORD, MASSACHUSETTS

A Wheel within a Wheel was first published by the
Fleming H. Revell Company in 1895.

ISBN: 978-1-55709-449-0

Thank you for purchasing an Applewood Book.
Applewood reprints America's lively classics—
books from the past that are of interest to modern
readers. For a free copy of our current catalog,
write to: Applewood Books, Box 365,
Bedford, MA 01730.

Printed in the United States of America

Library of Congress Cataloging-in-Publication Data
Willard, Frances Elizabeth, 1839–1898
    A wheel within a wheel / Frances Willard.
        p.   cm.
    Originally published: New York: F.H. Revell,
1895.
    ISBN: 978-1-55709-449-0
    1. Cycling for women.   2. Willard, Frances
Elizabeth, 1839–1898.   I. Title.
GV1057.W73 1997
796.6'082–dc21   97-1615
                           CIP

GRATEFULLY DEDICATED

TO

LADY HENRY SOMERSET,

WHO GAVE ME "GLADYS,"

THAT HARBINGER OF HEALTH AND HAPPINESS.

LIST OF ILLUSTRATIONS

PAGE

MISS WILLARD .... *Frontispiece*

A LACK OF BALANCE .... *facing page* 21

EASTNOR CASTLE 29

" SO EASY—WHEN YOU KNOW HOW".......... 36

" IT'S DOGGED AS DOES IT" 44

" LET GO—BUT STAND BY " 57

" AT LAST " 72

A WHEEL WITHIN A WHEEL

PRELIMINARY

FROM my earliest recollections, and up to the ripe age of fifty-three, I had been an active and diligent worker in the world. This sounds absurd; but having almost no toys except such as I could manufacture, my first plays were but the outdoor work of active men and women on a small scale. Born with an inveterate opposition to staying in the house, I very early learned to use a carpenter's kit and a gardener's tools, and followed in my mimic way the occupations of the poulterer and the farmer, working my little field with a wooden plow of my own making, and felling saplings with an ax rigged up from the old iron of the wagon-shop. Living in the country, far from the artificial restraints and conventions by which most girls are hedged from the activities that would develop a good physique, and endowed with the companionship of a mother who let me have my own sweet will, I " ran wild " until my sixteenth birthday, when the hampering long skirts were brought, with their accompanying corset and high heels; my hair was clubbed up with pins, and I remember writing in my journal, in the first heartbreak of a young human colt taken from its pleasant pasture, "Altogether, I recognize that my occupation is gone."

From that time on I always realized and was obedient to the limitations thus imposed, though in my heart of hearts I felt their unwisdom even more than their injustice. My work then changed from my beloved and breezy outdoor world to the indoor realm of study, teaching, writing, speaking, and went on almost without a break or pain until my fifty-third year, when the loss of my mother accentuated the strain of this long period in which mental and physical life were out of balance, and I fell into a mild form of what is called nerve-wear by the patient and nervous prostration by the lookers-on. Thus ruthlessly thrown out of the usual lines of reaction on my environment, and sighing for new worlds to conquer, I determined that I would learn the bicycle.

An English naval officer had said to me, after learning it himself, " You women have no idea of the new realm of happiness which the bicycle has opened to us men." Already I knew well enough that tens of thousands who could never afford to own, feed, and stable a horse, had by this bright invention enjoyed the swiftness of motion which is perhaps the most fascinating feature of material life, the charm of a wide outlook upon the natural world, and that sense of mastery which is probably the greatest attraction in horseback-riding. But the steed that never tires, and is

" mettlesome " in the fullest sense of the word, is full of tricks and capers, and to hold his head steady and make him prance to suit you is no small accomplishment. I had often mentioned in my temperance writings that the bicycle was perhaps our strongest ally in winning young men away from public-houses, because it afforded them a pleasure far more enduring, and an exhilaration as much more delightful as the natural is than the unnatural. From my observation of my own brother and hundreds of young men who have been my pupils, I have always held that a boy's heart is not set in him to do evil any more than a girl's, and that the reason our young men fall into evil ways is largely because we have not had the wit and wisdom to provide them with amusements suited to their joyous youth, by means of which they could invest their superabundant animal spirits in ways that should harm no one and help themselves to the best develop-ment and the cleanliest ways of living. So as a temperance reformer I always felt a strong attraction toward the bicycle, because it is the vehicle of so much harmless pleasure, and because the skill required in handling it obliges those who mount to keep clear heads and steady hands. Nor could I see a reason in the world why a woman should not ride the silent steed so swift and blithesome. I knew perfectly well that when, some ten or fifteen years ago, Miss Bertha von Hillern, a young German artist in America, took it into her head to give exhibitions of her skill in riding the bicycle she was thought by some to be a sort of semi-monster; and liberal as our people are in their views of what a woman may undertake, I should certainly have felt compromised, at that remote and benighted period, by going to see her ride, not because there was any harm in it, but solely because of what we call in homely phrase "the speech of people." But behold! it was long ago conceded that women might ride the tricycle—indeed, one had been presented to me by my friend Colonel Pope, of Boston, a famous manufacturer of these swift roadsters, as far back as 1886; and I had swung around the garden-paths upon its saddle a few minutes every evening when work was over at my Rest Cottage home.   I had even hoped to give an impetus among conservative women to this new line of physical development and outdoor happiness; but that is quite another story and will come in later.   Suffice it for the present that it did me good, as it doth the upright in heart, to notice recently that the Princesses Louise and Beatrice both ride the tricycle at Balmoral; for I know that with the great mass of feminine humanity this precedent will have exceeding weight—and where the tricycle prophesies the bicycle shall ere long preach the gospel of outdoors.

For we are all unconsciously the slaves of public opinion. When the hansom first came on London streets no woman having regard to her social state and standing would have dreamed of entering one of these pavement

gondoias unless accompanied by a gentleman
as her escort. But in course of time a few
women, of stronger individuality than the
average, ventured to go unattended; later
on, use wore off the glamour of the traditions
which said that women must not go alone,
and now none but an imbecile would hold
herself to any such observance.

A trip around the world by a young woman would have been regarded a quarter of
a century ago as equivalent to social out-
lawry; but now young women of the highest
character and talent are employed by leading
journals to whip around the world " on time,"
and one has done so in seventy-three, another in seventy-four days, while the young
women recently sent out by an Edinburgh
newspaper will no doubt considerably con-
tract these figures.

As I have mentioned, Fräulein von Hillern
is the first woman, so far as I know, who ever
rode a bicycle, and for this she was considered to be one of those persons who classified
nowhere, and who could not do so except to

the injury of the feminine guild with which they were connected before they " stepped out"; but now, in France, for a woman to ride a bicycle is not only " good form," but the current craze among the aristocracy.

Since Balaam's beast there has been but little authentic talking done by the four-footed; but that is no reason why the two-wheeled should not speak its mind, and the first utterance I have to chronicle in the softly flowing vocables of my bicycle is to the following purport.   I heard it as we trundled off down the Priory incline at the suburban home of Lady Henry Somerset, Reigate, England; it said: " Behold, I do not fail you; I am not a skittish beastie, but a sober, well-conducted roadster.   I did not ask you to mount or drive, but since you have done so you must now learn the laws of balance and exploitation. I did not invent these laws, but I have been built conformably to them, and you must suit yourself to the unchanging regulations of gravity, general and specific, as illustrated in

me.   Strange as the paradox may seem, you
will do this best by not trying to do it at all.
You must make up what you are pleased to
call your mind—make it up speedily, or you
will be cast in yonder mud-puddle, and no
blame to me and no thanks to yourself.   Two
things must occupy your thinking powers to
the exclusion of every other thing: first, the
goal; and, second, the momentum requisite
to reach it.   Do not look down like an imbecile upon the steering-wheel in front of
you—that would be about as wise as for a
nauseated voyager to keep his optical instru-
ments fixed upon the rolling waves.   It is
the curse of life that nearly every one looks
down.   But the microscope will never set
you free; you must glue your eyes to the
telescope for ever and a day.   Look up and
off and on and out; get forehead and foot
into line, the latter acting as a rhythmic spur
in the flanks of your equilibriated equine; so
shall you win, and that right speedily.

"It was divinely said that the kingdom of

God is within you.   Some make a mysticism
of this declaration, but it is hard common
sense; for the lesson you will learn from me is
this: every kingdom over which we reign must
be first formed within us on what the psychic
people call the ' astral plane,' but what I as a
bicycle look upon as the common parade-
ground of individual thought."

THE PROCESS

Courtiers wittily say that horseback riding
is the only thing in which a prince is apt to
excel, for the reason that the horse never
flatters and would as soon throw him as if he
were a groom.   Therefore it is only by actually mastering the art of riding that a prince
can hold his place with the noblest of the
four-footed animals.

Happily there is now another locomotive
contrivance which is no flatterer, and which
peasant and prince must master, if they do
this at all, by the democratic route of honest
hard work.   Well will it be for rulers when

the tough old Yorkshire proverb applies to
them as strictly as to the lowest of their sub-
jects: "*It's dogged as does it.*" We all know
the old saying, " Fire is a good servant, but
a bad master." This is equally true of the
bicycle: if you give it an inch—nay, a hair—it
will take an ell—nay, an evolution—and you a
contusion, or, like enough, a perforated knee-
cap.

Not a single friend encouraged me to learn
the bicycle except an active-minded young
school-teacher, Miss Luther, of my home-
town, Evanston, who came several times with
her wheel and gave me lessons. I also took
a few lessons in a stuffy, semi-subterranean
gallery in Chicago. But at fifty-three I was
at more disadvantage than most people, for
not only had I the impedimenta that result
from the unnatural style of dress, but I also
suffered from the sedentary habits of a life-
time. And then that small world (which is
our real one) of those who loved me best,
and who considered themselves largely re-

sponsible for my every-day methods of life, did not encourage me, but in their affectionate solicitude—and with abundant reason—thought I should "break my bones" and "spoil my future." It must be said, however, to their everlasting praise, that they opposed no objection when they saw that my will was firmly set to do this thing; on the contrary, they put me in the way of carrying out my purpose, and lent to my laborious lessons the light of their countenances reconciled. Actions speak so much louder than words that I here set before you what may be called a feminine bicycler's first position—at least it was mine.

Given a safety-bicycle—pneumatic tires and all the rest of it which renders the pneumatic safety the only safe Bucephalus—the gearing carefully wired in so that we shall not be entangled. "Woe is me!" was my first exclamation, naturally enough interpreted by my outriders "Whoa is me," and

A LACK OF BALANCE.

they "whoaed"—indeed, we did little else but "check up."

(Just here let me interpolate: Learn on a low machine, but "fly high" when once you have mastered it, as you have much more power over the wheels and can get up better speed with a less expenditure of force when you are above the instrument than when you are at the back of it. And remember this is as true of the world as of the wheel.)

The order of evolution was something like this: First, three young Englishmen, all strong-armed and accomplished bicyclers, held the machine in place while I climbed timidly into the saddle. Second, two well-disposed young women put in all the power they had, until they grew red in the face, off-setting each other's pressure on the cross-bar and thus maintaining the equipoise to which I was unequal. Third, one walked beside me, steadying the ark as best she could by holding the center of the deadly cross-bar, to let go whose handles meant chaos and collapse. After this I was able to hold my own if I had the moral support of my kind trainers, and it passed into a proverb among them, the short emphatic word of command I gave them at every few turns of the wheel: " Let go, but stand by." Still later everything was learned—how to sit, how to pedal, how to turn, how to dismount; but alas! how to vault into the saddle I found not; that was the coveted power that lingered long and would not yield itself.

That which caused the many failures I had in learning the bicycle had caused me failures in life; namely, a certain fearful looking for of judgment; a too vivid realization of the uncertainty of everything about me; an underlying doubt—at once, however (and this is all that saved me), matched and overcome by the determination not to give in to it.

The best gains that we make come to us after an interval of rest which follows strenuous endeavor. Having, as I hoped, mastered the rudiments of bicycling, I went away to Germany and for a fortnight did not even see the winsome wheel. Returning, I had the horse brought round, and mounted with no little trepidation, being assisted by one of my faithful guides; but behold! I found that in advancing, turning, and descending I was much more at home than when I had last exercised that new intelligence in the muscles which had been the result of repetitions resolutely attempted and practised long.

Another thing I found is that we carry in the mind a picture of the road; and if it is humpy by reason of pebbles, even if we steer clear of them, we can by no means skim along as happily as when its smoothness facilitates the pleasing impression on the retina; indeed, the whole science and practice of the bicycle is " in your eye " and in your will; the rest is mere manipulation.

As I have said, in many curious particulars the bicycle is like the world. When it had thrown me painfully once (which was the extent of my downfalls during the entire process of learning, and did not prevent me from resuming my place on the back of the treacherous creature a few minutes afterward), and more especially when it threw one of my dearest friends, hurting her knee so that it was painful for a month, then for a time Gladys had gladsome ways for me no longer, but seemed the embodiment of misfortune and dread. Even so the world has often seemed in hours of darkness and despondency; its iron mechanism, its pitiless grind, its swift, silent, on-rolling gait have oppressed to pathos, if not to melancholy. Good health and plenty of oxygenated air have promptly restored the equilibrium. But how many a fine spirit, to finest issues touched, has been worn and shredded by the world's mill until in desperation it flung itself away. We can easily carp at those who quit the crowded race-course without so much as saying " By your leave "; but " let him that thinketh he standeth take heed lest he fall." We owe it to nature, to nurture, to our environments, and, most of all, to our faith in God, that we, too, do not cry, like so many gentle hearts less brave and sturdy, "Anywhere, anywhere, out of the world."

Gradually, item by item, I learned the location of every screw and spring, spoke and tire, and every beam and bearing that went to make up Gladys. This was not the lesson of a day, but of many days and weeks, and it had to be learned before we could get on well together. To my mind the infelicities of which we see so much in life grow out of lack of time and patience thus to study and adjust the natures that have agreed in the sight of God and man to stand by one another to the last. They will not take the pains, they have not enough specific gravity, to balance themselves in their new environment. Indeed, I found a whole philosophy of life in the wooing and the winning of my bicycle.

Just as a strong and skilful swimmer takes

the waves, so the bicycler must learn to take such waves of mental impression as the passing of a gigantic hay-wagon, the sudden obtrusion of black cattle with wide-branching horns, the rattling pace of high-stepping steeds, or even the swift transit of a railway-train. At first she will be upset by the apparition of the smallest poodle, and not until she has attained a wide experience will she hold herself steady in presence of the critical eyes of a coach-and-four. But all this is a part of that equilibration of thought and action by which we conquer the universe in conquering ourselves.

I finally concluded that all failure was from a wobbling will rather than a wobbling wheel. I felt that indeed the will is the wheel of the mind—its perpetual motion having been learned when the morning stars sang together. When the wheel of the mind went well then the rubber wheel hummed merrily ; but specters of the mind there are as well as of the wheel. In the aggregate of perception concerning which we have reflected and from which we have deduced our generalizations upon the world without, within, above, there are so many ghastly and fantastical images that they must obtrude themselves at certain intervals, like filmy bits of glass in the turn of the kaleidoscope. Probably every accident of which I had heard or read in my half-century tinged the uncertainty that by the correlation of forces passed over into the tremor that I felt when we began to round the terminus bend of the broad Priory walk. And who shall say by what original energy the mind forced itself at once from the contemplation of disaster and thrust into the very movement of the foot on the pedal a concept of vigor, safety, and success? I began to feel that myself plus the bicycle equaled myself plus the world, upon whose spinning-wheel we must all learn to ride, or fall into the sluiceways of oblivion and despair. That which made me succeed with the bicycle was precisely what had gained me a measure of success in life—it was the hardihood of spirit that led me to begin, the persistence of will that held me to my task, and the patience that was willing to begin again when the last stroke had failed.   And so I found high moral uses in the bicycle and can commend it as a teacher without pulpit or creed.   He who succeeds, or, to be more exact in handing over my experience, she who succeeds in gaining the mastery of such an animal as Gladys, will gain the mastery of life, and by exactly the same methods and characteristics.

One of the first things I learned was that unless a forward impetus were given within well-defined intervals, away we went into the gutter, rider and steed.   And I said to myself: " It is the same with all reforms: sometimes they seem to lag, then they barely balance, then they begin to oscillate as if they would lose the track and tumble to one side; but all they need is a new impetus at the right moment on the right angle, and

EASTNOR CASTLE.

away they go again as merrily as if they had
never threatened to stop at all."

On the Castle terrace we went through a
long, narrow curve in a turret to seek a
broader esplanade. As we approached it I
felt wrought up in my mind, a little uncertain
in my motions; and for that reason, on a
small scale, my quick imagination put before
me pictures of a "standing from under" on
the part of the machine and damaging bruises
against the pitiless walls. But with a little
unobtrusive guiding by one who knew better
than I how to do it we soon came out of the
dim passage on to the broad, bright terrace
we sought, and in an instant my fears were
as much left behind as if I had not had them.
So it will be, I think, I hope—nay, I believe
—when, children that we are, we tremble on
the brink and fear to launch away; but we
shall find that death is only a bend in the
river of life that sets the current heavenward.

One afternoon, on the terrace at Eastnor
Castle—the most delightful bicycle gallery I

have found anywhere—I fell to talking with
a young companion about New-Year resolu-
tions. It was just before Christmas, but the
sky was of that moist blue that England only
knows, and the earth almost steamy in the
mild sunshine, while the soft outline of the
famous Malvern Hills was restful as the little
lake just at our feet, where swans were sail-
ing or anchoring according to their fancy.

One of us said: "I have already chosen
my motto for 1894, and it is this, from a
teacher who so often said to her pupils, when
meeting them in corridor or recitation-room,
'I have heard something nice about you,'
that it passed into a proverb in the school.
Now I have determined that my mental atti-
tude toward everybody shall be the same that
these words indicate. The meaning is iden-
tical with that of the inscription on the fire-
place in my den at home—'Let something
good be said.' I remember mentioning to
a literary friend that this was what I had
chosen, and so far was he from perceiving

my intention that he sarcastically remarked, 'Are you then afraid that people will say dull things unless you set this rule before them?' But my thought then was as it is now, that we should apply in our discussions of people and things the rule laid down by Coleridge, namely, 'Look for the good in everything that you behold and every person, but do not decline to see the defects if they are there, and to refer to them.'"

"That is an excellent motto," brightly replied the other, "but if we followed it life would not be nearly so amusing as it is now. I have several friends whose rule is never to say any harm of anybody, and to my mind this cripples their development, for the tendency of such a method is to dull one's powers of discrimination."

"But," said the first speaker, "would not a medium course be better?—such a one, for instance, as my motto suggests. This would not involve keeping silence about the faults of persons and things, but would de-

velop that cheerful atmosphere which helps
to smooth the rough edges of life, and at the
same time does not destroy the critical faculty,
because you are to tell the truth and the whole
truth concerning those around you, whereas
the common custom is to speak much of defects and little or not at all of merits."

"Yes," was the reply, "but it is not half
so entertaining to speak of virtues as of faults,
especially in this country; if you don't criti-
cize you can hardly talk at all, because the
English dwell a great deal on what we in
America call ' the selvage side ' of things."

" Have you, then, noticed this as a national
peculiarity after ten years of observation?"

"Yes; and I have often heard it remarked,
not only by our own countrymen, but by the
people here."

"What do you think explains it?"

"Well, I am inclined to apply the theory
of M. Taine, the great French critic, to most
of the circumstances of life, and I should say
it was the climate; its uncertainty, its con-

stant changes, the heaviness of the atmosphere, the amount of fog, the real stress and
strain to live that results from trying physical
conditions added to the razor-sharp edge of
business and social competition and the close
contact that comes of packing forty millions
of people of pronounced individuality on an
island no bigger than the State of Georgia.
To my mind the wonder is that they behave
so well!"

Once, when I grew somewhat discouraged
and said that I had made no progress for a
day or two, my teacher told me that it was
just so when she learned: there were grow-
ing days and stationary days, and she had
always noticed that just after one of these
last dull, depressing, and dubious intervals
she seemed to get an uplift and went ahead
better than ever. It was like a spurt in row-
ing. This seems to be the law of progress
in everything we do; it moves along a spiral
rather than a perpendicular; we seem to be
actually going out of the way, and yet it

turns out that we were really moving upward all the time.

One day, when my most expert trainer twisted the truth a little that she might encourage me, I was reminded of an anecdote.

In this practical age an illustration of the workings of truthfulness will often help a child more than any amount of exhortation concerning the theory thereof. For instance, a father in that level-headed part of the United States known as "out West" found that his little boy was falling into the habit of telling what was not true; so he said to him at the lunch-table, "Johnnie, I will come around with a horse and carriage at four o'clock to take you and mama for a drive this afternoon." The boy was in high spirits, and watched for his father at the gate; but the hours passed by until six o'clock, when that worthy appeared walking up the street in the most unconcerned manner; and when Johnnie, full of indignation and astonishment, asked him why he did not come as he had promised, the father said, "Oh, my boy, I just took it into my head that I would tell you a lie about the matter, just as you have begun telling lies to me." The boy began to cry with mingled disappointment and shame to think his father would do a thing like that; whereupon the father took the little fellow on his knee and said: "This has all been done to show you what mischief comes from telling what is not true. It spoils everybody's good time. If you cannot believe what I say and I cannot believe what you say, and nobody can believe what anybody says, then the world cannot go on at all; it would have to stop as the old eight-day clock did the other day, making us all late to dinner. It is only because, as a rule, we can believe in one another's word that we are able to have homes, do business, and enjoy life. Whoever goes straight on telling the truth helps more by that than he could in any other one way to build up the world into a beautiful and happy place; and every time anybody tells what is not true he helps to weaken everybody's confidence in everybody else, and to spoil the good time, not of himself alone, but of all those about him."

MY TEACHERS

I studied my various kind teachers with much care. One was so helpful that but for my protest she would fairly have carried me in her arms, and the bicycle to boot, the whole distance. This was because she had not a scintilla of knowledge concerning the machine, and she did not wish me to come to grief through any lack on her part.

Another was too timorous; the very twitter of her face, swiftly communicated to her arm and imparted to the quaking cross-bar, convulsed me with an inward fear; therefore, for her sake and mine, I speedily counted her out from the faculty in my bicycle college.

Another (and she, like most of my teachers, was a Londoner) was herself so capable, not to

"SO EASY—WHEN YOU KNOW HOW."

say adventurous, and withal so solicitous for
my best good, that she elicited my admiration
by her ingenious mixture of cheering me on
and holding me back; the latter, however,
predominated, for she never relinquished her
strong grasp on the cross-bar. She was a
fine, brave character, somewhat inclined to a
pessimistic view of life because of severe experience at home, which, coming to her at a
pitifully early period, when brain and fancy
were most impressionable, wrought an injustice to a nature large and generous—one
which under happier skies would have blos-
somed out into a perfect flower of woman-
hood. My offhand thinkings aloud, to which
I have always been greatly given, especially
when in genial company, she seemed to "catch
on the fly," as a reporter impales an idea on
his pencil-point. We had no end of what
we thought to be good talk of things in
heaven and earth and the waters under the
earth; of the mystery that lies so closely
round this cradle of a world, and all the

varied and ingenious ways of which the bicycle, so slow to give up its secret to a care-
worn and inelastic pupil half a century old,
was just then our whimsical and favorite
symbol.

We rejoiced together greatly in perceiving
the impetus that this uncompromising but
fascinating and illimitably capable machine
would give to that blessed "woman question" to which we were both devoted; for
we had earned our own bread many a year,
and she, although more than twenty years
my junior, had accumulated an amount of
experience well-nigh as great, because she
had lived in the world's heart, or the world's
carbuncle (just as one chooses to regard what
has been called in literary phrase the capital
of humanity).   We saw that the physical development of humanity's mother-half would
be wonderfully advanced by that universal
introduction of the bicycle sure to come
about within the next few years, because it
is for the interest of great commercial monop-

olies that this should be so, since if women patronize the wheel the number of buyers will be twice as large. If women ride they must, when riding, dress more rationally than they have been wont to do. If they do this many prejudices as to what they may be allowed to wear will melt away. Reason will gain upon precedent, and ere long the comfortable, sensible, and artistic wardrobe of the rider will make the conventional style of woman's dress absurd to the eye and unendurable to the understanding. A reform often advances most rapidly by indirection. An ounce of practice is worth a ton of theory; and the graceful and becoming costume of woman on the bicycle will convince the world that has brushed aside the theories, no matter how well constructed, and the arguments, no matter how logical, of dress-reformers.

A woman with bands hanging on her hips, and dress snug about the waist and chokingly tight at the throat, with heavily trimmed skirts dragging down the back and numerous folds heating the lower part of the spine, and with tight shoes, ought to be in agony. She ought to be as miserable as a stalwart man would be in the same plight. And the fact that she can coolly and complacently assert that her clothing is perfectly easy, and that she does not want anything more comfortable or convenient, is the most conclusive proof that she is altogether abnormal bodily, and not a little so in mind.

We saw with satisfaction the great advantage in good fellowship and mutual understanding between men and women who take the road together, sharing its hardships and rejoicing in the poetry of motion through landscapes breathing nature's inexhaustible charm and skyscapes lifting the heart from what is to what shall be hereafter. We discoursed on the advantage to masculine character of comradeship with women who were as skilled and ingenious in the manipulation of the swift steed as they themselves. We contended that whatever diminishes the sense

of superiority in men makes them more manly, brotherly, and pleasant to have about; we
felt sure that the bluff, the swagger, the bra-
vado of young England in his teens would not
outlive the complete mastery of the outdoor
arts in which his sister is now successfully
engaged. The old fables, myths, and follies
associated with the idea of woman's incom-
petence to handle bat and oar, bridle and rein,
and at last the cross-bar of the bicycle, are
passing into contempt in presence of the nim-
bleness, agility, and skill of " that boy's sister"; indeed, we felt that if she continued to
improve after the fashion of the last decade
her physical achievements will be such that it
will become the pride of many a ruddy youth
to be known as " that girl's brother." As we
discoursed of life, death, and the judgment to
come, of " man's inhumanity to man," as well
as to beasts, birds, and creeping things, we
frequently recurred to a phrase that has become habitual with me in these later years
when other worlds seem anchored close along-

side this, and when the telephone, the phono-
graph, and the microphone begin to show us
that every breath carries in itself not only the
power, but the scientific certainty of registra-
tion: "Well, one thing is certain: we shall
meet it in the ether."

One of my companions in the tribulation
of learning the bicycle, and the grace of its
mastery, was a tall, bright-faced, vigorous-
minded young Celt who is devoted to every
good word and work and has had much experience with the "submerged tenth," living
among them and trying to build character
among those waste places of humanity.   I
set out to teach this young woman the bicycle, and while she took her lesson—which,
as she is young, elastic, and long-limbed,
was vastly less difficult than mine—we talked
of many things: American women, and why
they do not walk; the English lower class,
and why they are less vigorous than the
Irish; the English girl of the slums, and why
she is less self-respecting than an Irish girl in

the same station. " There are many things for which we cannot account," said my young friend ; whereupon, with the self-elected mentorship of my half-century, I oracularly observed : " Cosmos has not a consequence without a cause; it is the business of reason to seek for causes, and, if it cannot make sure of them, to construct for itself theories as to what they are or will turn out to be when found. But the trouble is, when we have framed our theory, we come to look upon it as our child, that we have brought into the world, nurtured, and trained up by hand. The curse of life is that men will insist on holding their theories as true and imposing them on others; this gives rise to creeds, customs, constitutions, royalties, governments. Happy is he who knows that he knows nothing, or next to nothing, and holds his opinions like a bouquet of flowers in his hand, that sheds its fragrance everywhere, and which he is willing to exchange at any moment for one fairer and more sweet, instead of strapping them on like an armor of steel and thrusting with his lance those who do not accept his notions."

My last teacher was—as ought to be the case on the principle of climax—my best.   I think she might have given many a pointer to folks that bring up children, and I realized that no matter how one may think himself accomplished, when he sets out to learn a new language, science, or the bicycle he has entered a new realm as truly as if he were a child newly born into the world, and " Except ye become as little children " is the law by which he is governed.   Whether he will or not he must first creep, then walk, then run ; and the wisest guide he can have is the one who most studiously helps him to help himself.   This was a truism that I had heard all my life long, but never did a realizing sense of it settle down upon my spirit so thoroughly as when I learned the bicycle.   It is not the teacher who holds you in place by main strength that is going to help you win that

"IT'S DOGGED AS DOES IT."
Yorkshire Proverb.

elusive, reluctant, inevitable prize we call success, but it is the one who, while studiously
keeping in the background, steers you to the
fore. So No. 12 had the wit and wisdom to
retire to the rear of the saucy steed, that I
might form the habit of seeing no sign of aid
or comfort from any source except my own
reaction on' the treadles according to law;
yet cunningly contrived, by laying a skilled
hand upon the saddle without my observation, knowledge, or consent, to aid me in my
balancing. She diminished the weight thus
set to my account as rapidly as my own increasing courage and skill rendered this possible.

I have always observed—and not without
a certain pleasure, remembering my brother's
hardihood—that wherever a woman goes
some man has reached the place before her;
and it did not dim the verdure of my laurels
or the fullness of my content when I had
mastered Gladys to ascertain, from a letter
sent me by the wife of a man sixty-four

years of age who had just learned, that I was
" No. 2 " instead of " No. 1," thus obliging
me to rectify the frontier of chronology as I
had constructed it in relation to the conquest
of the bicycle; for I vainly thought that I
had fought the antics of Gladys as a sentry
on duty away out on the extreme frontier of
time.

But at last (which means in two months or
thereabouts, at ten or twenty minutes' practice off and on daily) I reached the goal, and
could mount the bicycle without the slightest
foreign interference or even the moral support of a sympathetic onlooker. In doing
this I realized that the totality of what I had
learned entered into the action. Every added
increment of power that I had gained in balancing, pedaling, steering, taking advantage
of the surfaces, adjusting my weight according to my own peculiarities, and so on, was
set to my account when I began to manage
the bulky steed that behaves worst of all
when a novice seeks the saddle and strikes

out alone. Just so, I felt, it had been all my life and will be, doubtless, in all worlds and with us all. The totality of native forces and acquired discipline and expert knowledge stands us in good stead for each crisis that we have to meet. There is a momentum, a cumulative power on which we can count in every new circumstance, as a capitalist counts upon his credit at the bank. It is not only a divine declaration, it is one of the basic laws of being, that " all things work *together* for good to them that love God "—that is, to them that are in love with God; and he who loves a law of God and makes himself obedient to that law has by that much loved God, only he does not always have the wit to know it.

The one who has learned latest and yet has really learned the mastery of the bicycle is the best teacher. Many a time I have heard boys in college say that it was not the famed mathematician who could teach them anything—he knew too much, he was too far ahead for them to hear his voice, he was impatient of their halting steps; but the tutor who had left college only the year before, and remembering his own failures and stupidity, had still that fellow-feeling that made him wondrous kind.

As has been stated, my last epoch consisted of learning to mount; that is the *pons asinorum* of the whole mathematical undertaking, for mathematical it is to a nicety. You have to balance your system more carefully than you ever did your accounts; not the smallest fraction can be out of the way, or away you go, the treacherous steed forming one half of an equation and yourself with a bruised knee forming the other. You must add a stroke at just the right angle to mount, subtract one to descend, divide them equally to hold your seat, and multiply all these movements in definite ratio and true proportion by the swiftest of all roots, or you will become the most minus of quantities. You must foot up your accounts with the strictest regularity;

there can be no partial payments in a business enterprise like this.

Although I could now mount and descend, turn corners and get over the ground all by myself, I still felt a lack of complete faith in Gladys, although she had never harmed me but once, and then it was my own fault in letting go the gleaming cross-bar, which is equivalent to dropping the bridle of a spirited steed. Let it be carefully remembered by every "beginning" bicycler that, whatever she forgets, she must forever keep her "main hold," else her horse is not bitted and will shy to a dead certainty.

As we grew better acquainted I thought how perfectly analogous were our relations to those of friends who became slowly seasoned one to the other: they have endured the vicissitudes of every kind of climate, of the changing seasons; they have known the heavy, water-logged conditions of spring, the shrinkage of summer's trying heat, the happy medium of autumn, and the contracting cold that winter brings; they are like the bits of wood, exactly apportioned and attuned, that go to make up a Stradivarius violin. They can count upon one another and not disagree, because the stress of life has molded them to harmony. They are like the well-worn robe, the easy shoe. There is no short road to this adjustment, so much to be desired; not any will win it short of "patient continuance in well-doing."

I noticed that the great law which I believe to be potential throughout the universe made no exception here: "According to thy faith be it unto thee" was the only law of success. When I felt sure that I should do my pedaling with judicial accuracy, and did not permit myself to dread the swift motion round a bend; when I formed in my mind the image of a successful ascent of the "Priory Rise"; when I fully purposed in my mind that I should not run into the hedge on the one side or the iron fence on the other, these prophecies were fulfilled with practical certainty.

I fell into the habit of varying my experience by placing before myself the image—so germane to the work in which I am engaged—of an inebriate in action, and accompanied this mental panorama by an orchestral effect of my own producing: " They reel to and fro, and stagger like a drunken man;" but could never go through this three consecutive times without lurching off the saddle. But when I put before me, as distinctly as my powers of concentration would permit, the image of my mother holding steadily above me a pair of balances, and looking at me with that quizzical expectant glance I knew so well, and saying: " Do it? Of course you'll do it; what else should you do?" I found that it was palpably helpful in enabling me to " sit straight and hold my own" on my uncertain steed. She always maintained, in the long talks we had concerning immortality, that the law I mention was conclusive, and was wont to close our conversations on that subject (in which I held the interrogative position) with some

such remark as this: " If Professor —— thinks
he is not immortal he probably is not; if I
think I am I may be sure I shall be, for is it
not written in the law, ' According to thy
faith be it unto thee'?"

Gradually I realized a consoling degree of
mastery over Gladys; but nothing was more
apparent to me than that we were not yet
thoroughly acquainted—we had not sum-
mered and wintered together.   I had not
learned her kinks, and she was as full of
them as the most spirited mare that sweeps
the course on a Kentucky race-track.   Although I have seen a race but once (and that
was in the Champs Élysées, Paris, a quarter of
a century ago), I am yet so much interested
in the fact that it is a Flora Temple, a Gold-
smith Maid, a Maud S., a Sunol, a California
Maid that often stands first on the record, that
I would fain have named my shying steed after
one of these; but as she was a gift from Lady
Henry Somerset this seemed invidious in me
as a Yankee woman, and so I called her

Gladys, having in view the bright spirit of the donor, the exhilarating motion of the machine, and the gladdening effect of its acquaintance and use on my health and disposition.

As I have said, I found from first to last that the process of acquisition exactly coincided with that which had given me everything I possessed of physical, mental, or moral success—that is, skill, knowledge, character. I was learning the bicycle precisely as I learned the a-b-c. When I set myself, as a stint, to mount and descend in regular succession anywhere from twenty to fifty times, it was on the principle that we do a thing more easily the second time than the first, the third time than the second, and so on in a rapidly increasing ratio, until it is done without any conscious effort whatever. This was precisely the way in which my mother trained me to tell the truth, and my music-teacher taught me that mastership of the piano keyboard which I have lost by disuse. Falling from grace may mean falling from a habit formed—how do we know? This opens a boundless field of ethical speculation which I would gladly have followed, but just then the steel steed gave a lurch as if to say, "Tend to your knitting"—the favorite expression of a Rocky Mountain stage-driver when tourists taxed him with questions while he was turning round a bend two thousand feet above the valley.

And now comes the question "What do the doctors say?" Here follow several testimonies:

" The question now of great interest to girls is in regard to the healthfulness of the wheel. Many are prophesying dire results from this fascinating exercise, and fond parents are refusing to allow their daughters to ride because they are girls. It will be a delight to girls to learn that the fact of their sex is, in itself, not a bar to riding a wheel. If the girl is normally constituted and is dressed hygienically, and if she will use judgment and not overtax herself in learning to ride, and in measuring the length of rides after she has learned, she is in no more danger from riding a wheel than is the young man. But if she persists in riding in a tight dress, and uses no judgment in deciding the amount of exercise she is capable of safely taking, it will be quite possible for her to injure herself, and then it is she, and not the wheel, that is to blame. Many physicians are now coming to regard the 'wheel' as beneficial to the health of women as well as of men."

Dr. Seneca Egbert says: " As an exercise bicycling is superior to most, if not all, others at our command. It takes one into the outdoor air; it is entirely under control; can be made gentle or vigorous as one desires; is active and not passive; takes the rider outside of himself and the thoughts and cares of his daily work; develops his will, his attention, his courage and independence, and makes pleasant what is otherwise most irksome. Moreover, the exercise is well and equally distributed over almost the whole

body, and, as Parker says, when all the muscles are exercised no muscle is likely to be
over-exercised."

He advocates cycling as a remedy for dys-
pepsia, torpid liver, incipient consumption,
nervous exhaustion, rheumatism, and melan-
cholia.   In regard to the exercise for women
he says: " It gets them out of doors, gives
them a form of exercise adapted to their
needs, that they may enjoy in company with
others or alone, and one that goes to the root
of their nervous troubles."

He instances two cases, of girls fourteen
and eighteen years of age, where a decided
increase in height could be fairly attributed to
cycling.

The question is often asked if riding a wheel
is not the same as running a sewing-machine.
Let the same doctor answer: " Not at all.
Women, at least, sit erect on a wheel, and
consequently the thighs never make even a
right angle with the trunk, and there is no
stasis of blood in the lower limbs and geni-

"LET GO—BUT STAND BY."

talia. Moreover, the work itself makes the rider breathe in oceans of fresh air; while the woman at the sewing-machine works indoors, stoops over her work, contracting the chest and almost completely checking the flow of blood to and from the lower half of her body, where at the same time she is increasing the demand for it, finally aggravating the whole trouble by the pressure of the lower edge of the corset against the abdomen, so that the customary congestions and displacements have good cause for their existence."

" The great desideratum in all recreations is pure air, plenty of it, and lungs free to absorb it." (Dr. Lyman B. Sperry.)

" Let go, but stand by "—this is the golden rule for parent and pastor, teacher and friend; the only rule that at once respects the individuality of another and yet adds one's own, so far as may be, to another's momentum in the struggle of life.

How difficult it is for the trainer to judge

exactly how much force to exercise in help-
ing to steer the wheel and start the wheeler
along the macadamized highway! In this
the point of view makes all the difference.
The trainer is tall, the rider short; the first
can poise on the off-treadle while one foot
is on the ground, but the last must learn to
balance while one foot is in the air. For
one of these perfectly to comprehend the
other's relation to the vehicle is practically
impossible; the degree to which he may at-
tain this depends upon the amount of imagination to the square inch with which he has
been fitted out. The opacity of the mind,
its inability to project itself into the realm of
another's personality, goes a long way to explain the friction of life. If we would set
down other people's errors to this rather than
to malice prepense we should not only get
more good out of life and feel more kindly
toward our fellows, but doubtless the recti-
tude of our intellects would increase, and the
justice of our judgments. For instance, it is

my purpose, so far as I understand myself, to be considerate toward those about me; but my pursuits have been almost purely mental, and to perceive what would seem just to one whose pursuits have been almost purely mechanical would require an act of imagination of which I am wholly incapable. We are so shut away from one another that none tells those about him what he considers ideal treatment on their part toward him. He thinks about it all the same, mumbles about it to himself, mutters about it to those of his own guild, and these mutterings make the discontent that finally breaks out in reforms whose tendency is to distribute the good things of this life more equally among the living. But nothing will probe to the core of this the greatest disadvantage under which we labor—that is, mutual non-comprehension—except a basis of society and government which would make it easy for each to put himself in another's place because his place is so much like another's. We shall be less imaginative, perhaps, in those days—the critics say this is inevitable; but it will only be because we need less imagination in order to do that which is just and kind to every one about us.

In my early home my father always set us children to work by stints—that is, he measured off a certain part of the garden to be weeded, or other work to be done, and when we had accomplished it our working-hours were over. With this deeply ingrained habit in full force I set myself stints with the bicycle. In the later part of my novitiate fifty attempts a day were allotted to that most difficult of all achievements, learning to mount, and I calculate that five hundred such efforts well put in will solve that most intricate problem of specific gravity.

Now concerning falls: I set out with the determination not to have any. Though mentally adventurous I have always been physically cautious; a student of physiology in my youth, I knew the reason why I

brought so much less elasticity to my task
than did my young and agile trainers. I
knew the penalty of broken bones, for these
a tricycle had cost me some years before.
My trainers were kind enough to encourage
me by saying that if I became an expert in
slow riding I should take the rapid wheel as
a matter of course and thus be really more
accomplished (in the long run as well as the
short) than by any other process. So I have
had but one real downfall to record as the
result of my three months' practice, and it
illustrates the old saying that "pride goeth
before destruction, and a haughty spirit before a fall"; for I was not a little lifted up by
having learned to dismount with confidence
and ease—I will not say with grace, for at
fifty-three that would be an affectation—so
one bright morning I bowled on down the
Priory drive waving my hand to my most
adventurous aide-de-camp, and calling out
as I left her behind, "Now you will see
how nicely I can do it—watch!" when be-

hold! that timid left foot turned traitor, and
I came down solidly on my knee, and the
knee on a pebble as relentless as prejudice
and as opinionated as ignorance. The nervous shock made me well-nigh faint, the bicycle tumbled over on my prone figure, and
I wished I had never heard of Gladys or of
any wheel save

> " Fly swiftly round, ye wheels of time,
> And bring the welcome day—"

of my release into the ether.

Let me remark to any young woman who
reads this page that for her to tumble off her
bike is inexcusable. The lightsome elasticity
of every muscle, the quickness of the eye, the
agility of motion, ought to preserve her from
such a catastrophe. I have had no more falls
simply because I would not. I have pro-
ceeded on a basis of the utmost caution, and
aside from that one pitiful performance the
bicycle has cost me hardly a single bruise.

AN ETHEREAL EPISODE

They that know nothing fear nothing.
Away back in 1886 my alert young friend,
Miss Anna Gordon, and my ingenious young
niece, Miss Katharine Willard, took to the
tricycle as naturally as ducks take to water.
The very first time they mounted they went
spinning down the long shady street, with its
pleasant elms, in front of Rest Cottage, where
for nearly a generation mother and I had had
our home. Even as the war-horse snuffeth
the battle from afar, I longed to go and do likewise. Remembering my country bringing-
up and various exploits in running, climbing,
horseback-riding, to say nothing of my tame
heifer that I trained for a Bucephalus, I said
to myself, " If those girls can ride without
learning so can I!" Taking out my watch
I timed them as they, at my suggestion, set
out to make a record in going round the
square. Two and a half minutes was the result. I then started with all my forces well

in hand, and flew around in two and a quarter minutes. Not contented with this, but puffed up with foolish vanity, I declared that I would go around in two minutes; and, encouraged by their cheers, away I went without a fear till the third turning-post was reached, when the left hand played me false, and turning at an acute angle, away I went sidelong, machine and all, into the gutter, ·falling on my right elbow, which felt like a glassful of chopped ice, and I knew that for the first time in a life full of vicissitudes I had been really hurt. Anna Gordon's white face as she ran toward me caused me to wave my uninjured hand and call out, " Never mind!" and with her help I rose and walked into the house, wishing above all things to go straight to my own room and lie on my own bed, and thinking as I did so how pathetic is that instinct that makes " the stricken deer go weep," the harmed hare seek the covert.

Two physicians were soon at my side, and my mother, then over eighty years of age,

came in with much controlled agitation and
seated herself beside my bed, taking my hand
and saying, " O Frank! you were always too
adventurous."

Our family physician was out of town, and
the two gentlemen were well-nigh strangers.
It was a kind face, that of the tall, thin man
who looked down upon me in my humilia-
tion, put his ear against my heart to see if
there would be any harm in administering
ether, handled my elbow with a woman's
gentleness, and then said to his assistant,
" Now let us begin."   And to me who had
been always well, and knew nothing of such
unnatural proceedings, he remarked, "Breathe
into the funnel—full, natural breaths; that is
all you have to do."

I set myself to my task, as has been my
wont always, and soon my mother and my
friend, Anna Gordon, who were fanning me
with big "palm-leaves," became grotesque
and then ridiculous, and I remember saying
(or at least I remember that I once remem-

bered), " You are a couple of enormous crick-
ets standing on your hind legs, and you have
each a spear of dry grass, and you look as
if you were paralyzed; and you wave your
withered spears of grass, and you call that
fanning a poor woman who is suffocating
before your eyes." I labored with them, en-
treated them, and dealt with them in great
plainness—so much so that my mother could
not bear to hear me talk in such a foolish
fashion, and quietly withdrew to her own
room, closed the door, and sat down to pos-
sess her soul in patience until the operation
should be over.

Then the scene changed, and as they put
on the splints pain was involved, and I heard
those about me laughing in the most unfeel-
ing manner while I murmured: " She always
believed in humanity—she always said she
did and would; and she has lived in this town
thirty years, and they are hurting her—they
are hurting her dreadfully; and if they keep
on she will lose her faith in human nature,

and if she should it will be the greatest calam-
ity that can happen to a human being."

Now the scene changed once more—I was
in the starry heavens, and said to the young
friends who had come in and stood beside
me: "Here are stars as thick as apples on a
bough, and if you are good you shall each
have one.   And, Anna, because you *are*
good, and always have been, you shall be
given a whole solar system to manage just as
you like.   The Heavenly Father has no end
of them; He tosses them out of His hand as
a boy does marbles; He spins them like a
cocoon; He has just as many after He has
given them away as He had before He
began."

Then there settled down upon me the
most vivid and pervading sense of the love
of God that I have ever known.   I can give
no adequate conception of it, and what I said,
as my comrades repeated it to me, was something after this order:

    "We are like blood-drops floating through

the great heart of our Heavenly Father. We are infinitely safe, and cared for as tenderly as a baby in its mother's arms. No harm can come anywhere near us; what we call harm will turn out to be the very best and kindest way of leading us to be our best selves. There is no terror in the universe, for God is always at the center of everything. He is love, as we read in the good book, and He has but one wish—that we should love one another; in Him we live, and move, and have our being."

Little by little, freeing my mind of all sorts of queer notions, I came back out of the only experience of the kind that I have ever known; but I must say that had I not learned the great evils that result from using anesthetics I should have wished to try ether again, just for the ethical and spiritual help that came to me. It let me out into a new world, greater, more mellow, more godlike, and it did me no harm at all.

During the time my arm was in a sling I

" sat about "—something not easy to do for
one of active mind and life. I learned to
write with my left hand—for this was before
the happy days of the many stenographers—
and my hieroglyphics went out to all the
leading temperance women of this country.
One morning the bell, distant and musical,
tolled in the steeple of the university. We
knew it meant that General Grant was dead,
for the newspapers and despatches of the
previous evening had prepared us. Some-
how a deep chord in my soul vibrated to the
tone of the bell—a chord of patriotism—and I
went away to the vine-covered piazza, where
I was wont to sit, and in twenty minutes
(which fact is my apology for their limping
feet) wrote out my heart in the following lines.
They had at least the merit of sincere devo-
tion, and were telephoned to Chicago, eleven
miles away, by Anna Gordon, and appearing
in the daily *Inter-Ocean* were read at their
breakfast-tables by many other patriots next
morning. I do not know when anything has

given me more real pleasure than to be told
that a stalwart soldier belonging to the Grand
Army of the Republic read my crude but
heartfelt lines aloud to his wife and daughter,
and at the close brushed away a manly tear.

GRANT IS DEAD.

*On Hearing the University Bell at Evanston, Ill., Toll for
the Death of General Grant at Nine O'clock A.M.,
July 23, 1885.*

> Toll, bells, from every steeple,
> Tell the sorrow of the people;
> Moan, sullen guns, and sigh
> For the greatest who could die.
>   Grant is dead.

> Never so firm were set those moveless lips as now,
> Never so dauntless shone that massive brow;
> The silent man has passed into the silent tomb.
>   Ring out our grief, sweet bell,
>   The people's sorrow tell
> For the greatest who could die.
>   Grant is dead.

> " Let us have peace!" Great heart,
>   That peace has come to thee;
> Thy sword for freedom wrought,
>   And now thy soul is free,
> While a rescued nation stands
>   Mourning its fallen chief—

The Southern with the Northern lands,
  Akin in honest grief.
The hands of black and white
  Shall clasp above thy grave,
Children of the Republic all,
  No master and no slave.
Almost " all summer on this line "
Thou steadily didst " fight it out ";
But Death, the silent,
Matched at last our silent chief,
And put to rout his brave defense.
  Moan, sullen guns, and sigh
  For the bravest who could die.
      Grant is dead.

The huge world holds to-day
  No fame so great, so wide,
As his whose steady eyes grew dim
  On Mount McGregor's side
Only an hour ago, and yet
The whole great world has learned
      That Grant is dead.

O heart of Christ! what joy
Brings earth's new brotherhood!
All lands as one,
Buckner, Grant's bed beside,
The priest and Protestant in converse kind;
Prayers from all hearts, and Grant
Praying " we all might meet in better worlds."
  Toll, bells, from every steeple,
  Tell the sorrow of the people;
  So true in life, so calm and strong,
  Bravest of all, in death suffering so long

And without one complaint!
Moan, sullen guns, and sigh
For the greatest who could die;
Salute the nation's head.
Our Grant is dead.

IN CONCLUSION

If I am asked to explain why I learned the
bicycle I should say I did it as an act of grace,
if not of actual religion. The cardinal doctrine
laid down by my physician was, " Live out of
doors and take congenial exercise;" but from
the day when, at sixteen years of age, I was
enwrapped in the long skirts that impeded
every footstep, I have detested walking and
felt with a certain noble disdain that the conventions of life had cut me off from what in
the freedom of my prairie home had been
one of life's sweetest joys. Driving is not
real exercise; it does not renovate the river
of blood that flows so sluggishly in the veins
of those who from any cause have lost the
natural adjustment of brain to brawn. Horseback-riding, which does promise vigorous exercise, is expensive. The bicycle meets all

"AT LAST."

the conditions and will ere long come within the reach of all. Therefore, in obedience to the laws of health, I learned to ride. I also wanted to help women to a wider world, for I hold that the more interests women and men can have in common, in thought, word, and deed, the happier will it be for the home. Besides, there was a special value to women in the conquest of the bicycle by a woman in her fifty-third year, and one who had so many comrades in the white-ribbon army that her action would be widely influential. Then there were three minor reasons:

I did it from pure natural love of adventure—a love long hampered and impeded, like a brook that runs underground, but in this enterprise bubbling up again with somewhat of its pristine freshness and taking its merry course as of old.

Second, from a love of acquiring this new implement of power and literally putting it underfoot.

Last, but not least, because a good many people thought I could not do it at my age.

It is needless to say that a bicycling costume was a prerequisite. This consisted of
a skirt and blouse of tweed, with belt, rolling
collar, and loose cravat, the skirt three inches
from the ground; a round straw hat, and
walking-shoes with gaiters. It was a simple,
modest suit, to which no person of common
sense could take exception.

As nearly as I can make out, reducing the
problem to actual figures, it took me about
three months, with an average of fifteen minutes' practice daily, to learn, first, to pedal;
second, to turn; third, to dismount; and
fourth, to mount independently this most
mysterious animal. January 20th will always
be a red-letter bicycle day, because although
I had already mounted several times with no
hand on the rudder, some good friend had
always stood by to lend moral support; but
summoning all my force, and, most forcible
of all, what Sir Benjamin Ward Richardson
declares to be the two essential elements—de-
cision and precision—I mounted and started

off alone. From that hour the spell was broken; Gladys was no more a mystery: I had learned all her kinks, had put a bridle in her teeth, and touched her smartly with the whip of victory. Consider, ye who are of a considerable chronology: in about thirteen hundred minutes, or, to put it more mildly, in twenty-two hours, or, to put it most mildly of all, in less than a single day as the almanac reckons time—but practically in two days of actual practice—amid the delightful surroundings of the great outdoors, and inspired by the bird-songs, the color and fragrance of an English posy-garden, in the company of devoted and pleasant comrades, I had made myself master of the most remarkable, ingenious, and inspiring motor ever yet devised upon this planet.

Moral: *Go thou and do likewise!*

CPSIA information can be obtained at www.ICGtesting.com
Printed in the USA
LVOW12s2208140813

347979LV00001B/21/P

9 781557 094490